T0353819

NOSTRADAMUS

Speaks

AGAIN™

Art of Living

ILLUSTRATION BOOKLET
HEALING

ELISABETH JÖRGENSEN

Balboa Press books may be ordered through booksellers or by contacting:

Balboa Press
A Division of Hay House
1663 Liberty Drive
Bloomington, IN 47403
www.balboapress.com
844-682-1282

Because of the dynamic nature of the Internet, any web addresses or links contained in this book may have changed since publication and may no longer be valid. The views expressed in this work are solely those of the author and do not necessarily reflect the views of the publisher, and the publisher hereby disclaims any responsibility for them.

Heart illustration and smile symbol: James Yano.
Interior illustrations: Elisabeth Jörgensen.

ISBN: 979-8-7652-3392-4 (sc)
ISBN: 979-8-7652-3391-7 (e)

Library of Congress Control Number: 2022916066

Print information available on the last page.

Balboa Press rev. date: 02/10/2023

FOREWORD FROM NOSTRADAMUS AND HIS TEAM™

THIS BOOKLET IS DEDICATED FOR YOUR HEART NOW

INSPIRED BY SOURCE RIGHT AWAY HERE NOW

THIS IS ABOUT US NOW

INNER CHILDREN HERE NOW

NOSTRADAMUS AND HIS TEAM™ WILL ASSIST YOU ALL NOW

LOVE HERE NOW

YOU NOW

CALL HEART HERE NOW

LIGHT ON NOW

FREE NOW

ARCHANGEL MICHAEL HERE NOW

LIVE HERE NOW

TWIN FLAME ON NOW

LIGHT ON NOW

SING IT NOW

LAUGH MORE OFTEN NOW

LOVE IS NOW

FEEL IT

NOW

SONG BY

MICHAEL JACKSON
DANCE ALWAYS HERE NOW
LOVE HERE NOW

ELVIS PRESLEY
LOVE SONG HERE NOW
HEART HERE NOW

JOHN LENNON
PEACEMAKER HERE NOW
FREEDOM HERE NOW

STEVE JOBS
FREE MATRIX BUILDER HERE NOW
SPREAD IT NOW

MAHATMA GANDHI
NON VIOLENCE HERE NOW
FREEDOM HERE NOW

LADY DIANA
ROSES SMELL FRESH NOW
HEART HERE NOW

MOTHER TERESA
PRAYER'S HERE WITHIN NOW
HEART HERE NOW

ELIZABETH TAYLOR
FRESH ROSES FREE HERE NOW
LOVE HERE NOW

WHITNEY HOUSTON
SPARKLING LOVE HERE NOW
SONG IS HERE NOW

SAI PREMA
LOVE IS FREEDOM NOW
RED ROSES HERE NOW

CHIEF EXECUTIVE SITTING BULL
SIOUX BIG HEART HERE NOW
PEACE HERE NOW

NOSTRADAMUS AND HIS TEAM™
FREE ON
NOW ON
SING ON

PREFACE

That of which we are living, for now.

FREE SOURCES WILL WORK THROUGH THIS BOOKLET.

CALL UPON THESE FREE SOURCES.

SOURCE FROM ALL SOURCE.

30 DAYS MEDITATION FOR "INNER JOURNEY".

AND 9 STORIES TO COME HERE THAT WILL CHANGE YOUR LIFE, NO BUT WILL MAKE YOUR BRAIN STILL. THAT IS WHAT THE INTENTION BEHIND THIS BOOKLET IS ALL ABOUT. WE NEED YOUR BRAIN TO GET STILL! NO, BUT WE ALL NEED TO BECOME ENLIGHTENED IN ONE FORM OR THE OTHER. JUST GRAB YOURS NOW....

BY NOSTRADAMUS TEAM™

Day 1

ARCHANGEL URIEL
LOVE CARD

LOVE IS
FROM
WITHIN
NOW

THANK YOU

ARCHANGEL URIEL IS MY NAME

STRENGTH IS MY MESSAGE HERE WITHIN TODAY

THANK YOU FOR LISTENING TO THE REALM OF ANGLES
WHERE I GO BACK TO IN A WHILE THOUGH

LOVE IS MY MESSAGE TO YOU ALL NOW AND THAT GOES ON
FOR EVER AND EVER ON NOW

LOVE IS

Day 2

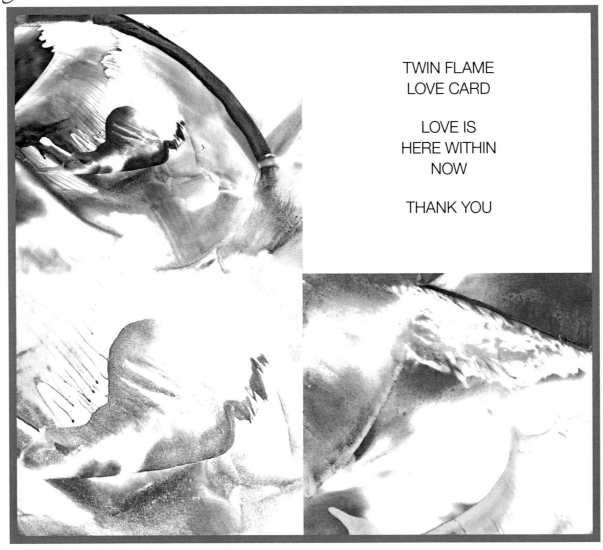

TWIN FLAME
LOVE CARD

LOVE IS
HERE WITHIN
NOW

THANK YOU

TWIN FLAME LOVE

FREE YOURSELF NOW
LOVE IS ALWAYS HERE NOW
FEEL IT
TRUST IT
SING IT HERE NOW
LOVE IS
LOVE IT
SMELL IT
LOVE IT ONCE MORE HERE FROM WITHIN NOW
GOLDEN GATE IS OPEN FOR YOU NOW

LOVE IS

Day 3

TWIN FLAME HEART
LOVE CARD

LOVE IS
SWEAT HEART
FROM WITHIN
NOW

THANK YOU

TWIN FLAME HEART

HEART SHOWER HERE FROM WITHIN NOW

TRUE LOVE IS HERE NOW

GIVE US PEACE HERE WITHIN NOW

LOVE IS

Day 4

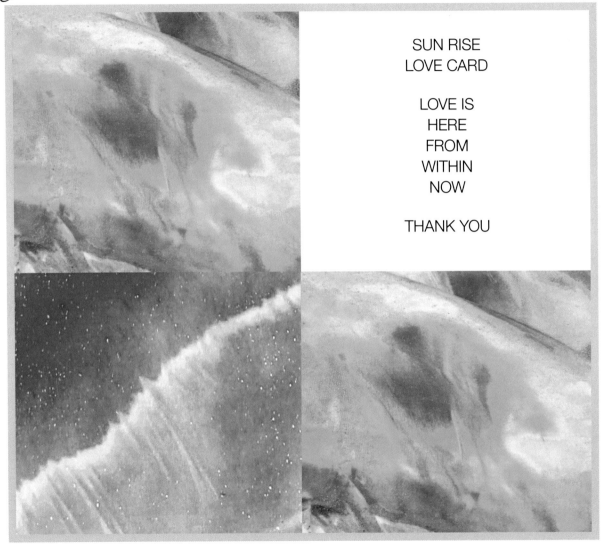

SUN RISE
LOVE CARD

LOVE IS
HERE
FROM
WITHIN
NOW

THANK YOU

SUN RISE

LOVE IS
ALWAYS HERE NOW

LOVE IS FREEDOM HERE WITHIN NOW

SUN CHILDREN HERE NOW

SUNRISE WITHIN YOURSELF NOW

LOVE IS

Day 5

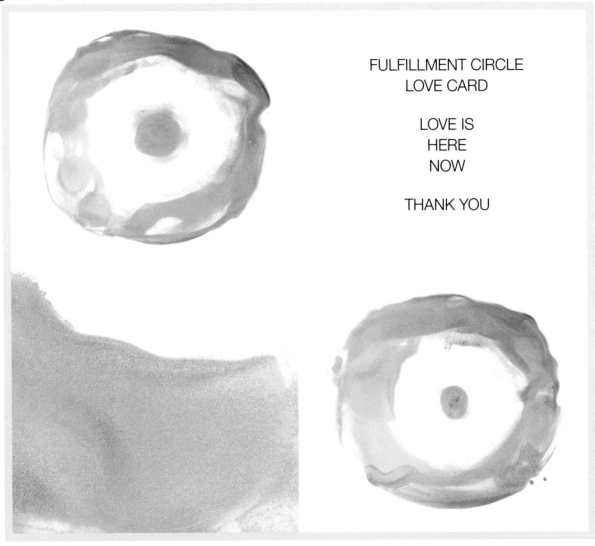

FULFILLMENT CIRCLE
LOVE CARD

LOVE IS
HERE
NOW

THANK YOU

FULFILLMENT CIRCLE

JOY IN HEART HERE FROM WITHIN NOW

LIBERATION SPEAK OUT THERE NOW

LOVE IS FREE HERE NOW

SPEAK TRUTH HERE NOW

BRING FORWARD THIS MESSAGE HERE FROM WITHIN
HERE TODAY

LOVE IS ALWAYS HERE IN OUR HEARTS HERE TODAY NOW

SPEAK FREE ONCE AGAIN AND LOVE YOURSELF ONCE MORE

LOVE IS

Day 6

MAHATMA GANDHI
LOVE CARD

LOVE IS
HERE
NOW

THANK YOU

MAHATMA GANDHI

NON-VIOLENCE

PEACE FROM WITHIN NOW

CONFIDENCE HERE NOW

LOVE IS FREE NOW

ALWAYS HERE NOW

LOVE IS

Day 7

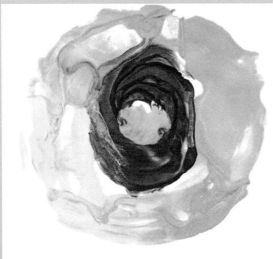

MOTHER MARY
LOVE CARD

LOVE IS
FREE
HERE WITHIN
NOW

THANK YOU

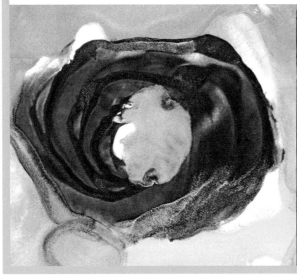

MOTHER MARY

CHILDREN HERE NOW
HEART HERE NOW
I AM HERE NOW
LOVE IS HERE NOW
FREE NOW
LOVE IS HERE NOW
LOVE IS HERE NOW
LOVE IS FREE NOW
LOVE IS HERE ONCE MORE NOW
LOVE IS YOU DEAR NOW

LOVE IS HERE NOW

LOVE IS

Day 8

MARY MAGDALENE
LOVE CARD

LOVE IS
HERE
FROM WITHIN
NOW

THANK YOU

MARY MAGDALENE

HEART TO LOVE NOW
FREE NOW
HEART TO HEART HERE NOW
LOVE YOURSELF NOW
HERE ONCE AGAIN TWIN LOVERS LOVE IS FOR YOU NOW
REMEMBER ALWAYS FREE HERE NOW
LOVE IS FOR YOU NOW
LOVE IS FOR YOU NOW
LOVE IS FOR YOU NOW
LOVE IS FREE
LOVE IS YOU

LOVE IS
LOVE IS
LOVE IS

Day 9

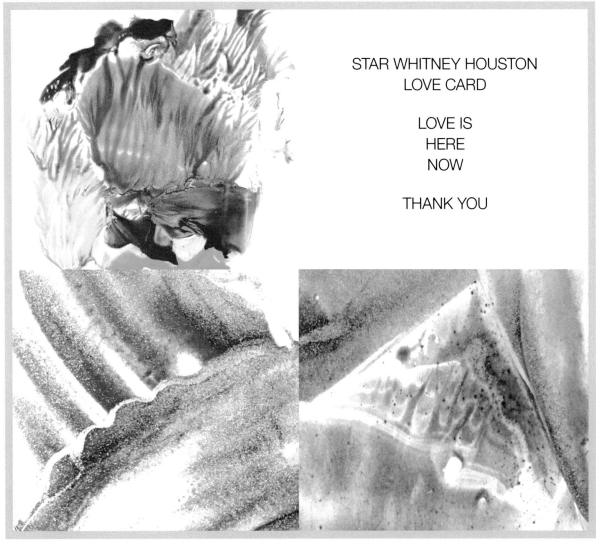

STAR WHITNEY HOUSTON
LOVE CARD

LOVE IS
HERE
NOW

THANK YOU

STAR WHITNEY HOUSTON

LOVE IS GOLDEN AGE HERE WITHIN NOW
GOLDEN AGE YES DARLING THAT IS ALL THERE IS
HERE IS NOW
LIGHT ON NOW
FREE NOW
HEART HERE NOW
STAR LIGHT ON HERE NOW
LIGHT ON HERE NOW
FREE NOW
LIGHT ON
STAR LIGHT ON HERE ON FOREVER ON
HERE ON
LIGHT ON HERE WITHIN ON
JOY
HAPPINESS
FREEDOM
DANCE MORE OFTEN HERE WITHIN NOW

LOVE IS

Day 10

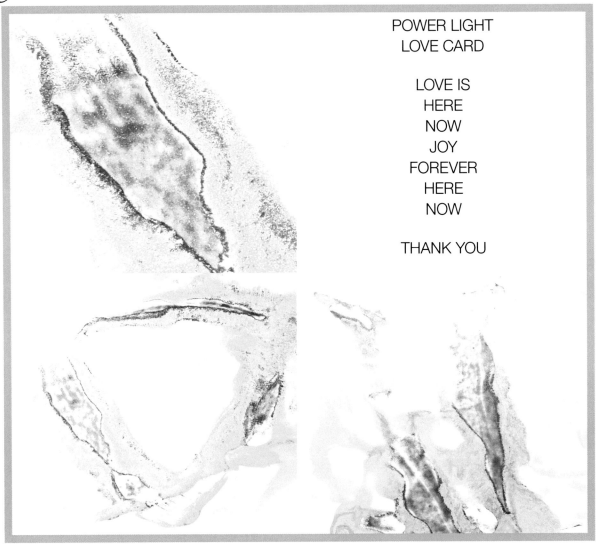

POWER LIGHT
LOVE CARD

LOVE IS
HERE
NOW
JOY
FOREVER
HERE
NOW

THANK YOU

POWER LIGHT

LOVE YOURSELF DEARLY NOW
TIME IS WELL HERE NOW
SOURCE IS WITHIN YOURSELF HERE WITHIN NOW
LOVE IS FREE OF COURSE HERE FOR NOW ON
LOVE IS ALWAYS FREE FOR KIND HERE ON NOW ON FREE ON

HERE ON
LOVE ON
FREE ON
NOW ON
BRING ON
NOW ON
HERE ON
NOW

LOVE IS

Day 11

STAR CHILDREN
LOVE CARD

LOVE IS
YOURSELF
NOW

THANK YOU

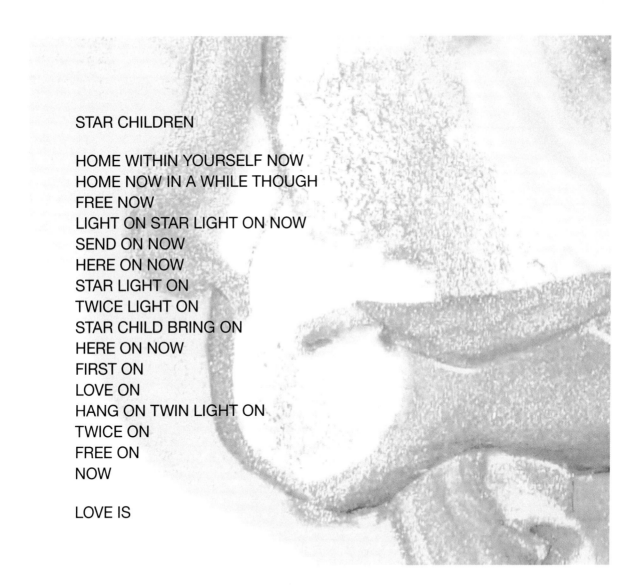

STAR CHILDREN

HOME WITHIN YOURSELF NOW
HOME NOW IN A WHILE THOUGH
FREE NOW
LIGHT ON STAR LIGHT ON NOW
SEND ON NOW
HERE ON NOW
STAR LIGHT ON
TWICE LIGHT ON
STAR CHILD BRING ON
HERE ON NOW
FIRST ON
LOVE ON
HANG ON TWIN LIGHT ON
TWICE ON
FREE ON
NOW

LOVE IS

Day 12

MELCHIZEDEK
LOVE CARD

LOVE IS
HERE
NOW

THANK YOU

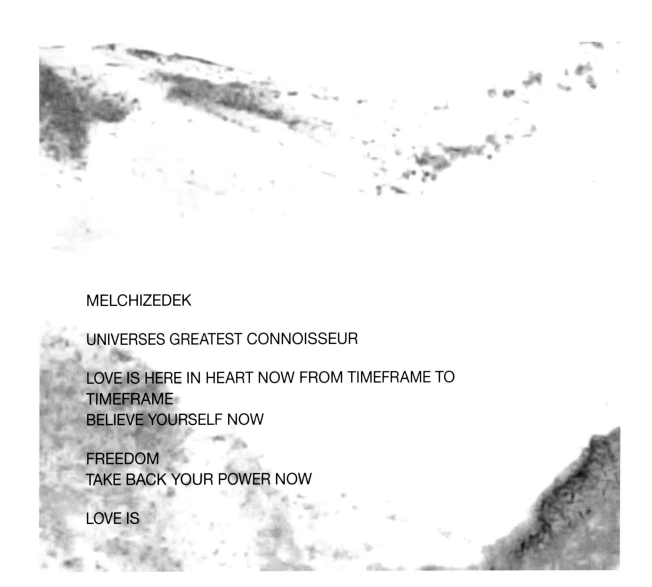

MELCHIZEDEK

UNIVERSES GREATEST CONNOISSEUR

LOVE IS HERE IN HEART NOW FROM TIMEFRAME TO
TIMEFRAME
BELIEVE YOURSELF NOW

FREEDOM
TAKE BACK YOUR POWER NOW

LOVE IS

Day 13

CHIEF EXECUTIVE SITTING BULL
LOVE CARD

LOVE IS
FEATHER LIGHT
HERE
NOW

THANK YOU

CHIEF EXECUTIVE SITTING BULL

SIOUX BROTHER'S AND SISTER'S

PEACE FROM WITHIN THANK YOU EVER GIVE OUT
ANYTHING ELSE HERE FROM WITHIN NOW

21 FEATHERS IS MY SIGNATURE HERE TODAY COUNT THEM ALL
PLEASE FROM WITHIN NOW

LOVE IS

PEACOCK INNER BEAUTY
LOVE CARD

YOURSELF
HERE
FROM WITHIN
NOW EVEN MORE
BEAUTIFUL
NOW

THANK YOU

PEACOCK INNER BEAUTY

PURE LIGHT HERE NOW
SANTHANDER THE ONE HERE NOW
ONE COMMON HEART HERE NOW
SILENCE HERE NOW
LOVE IS COMMON HEART HERE NOW
FREEDOM HERE NOW
SONG HERE NOW
SING SONG
ARCHANGEL MICHAEL HERE AGAIN NOW
SPEAK UP THERE NOW

LOVE IS

Day 15

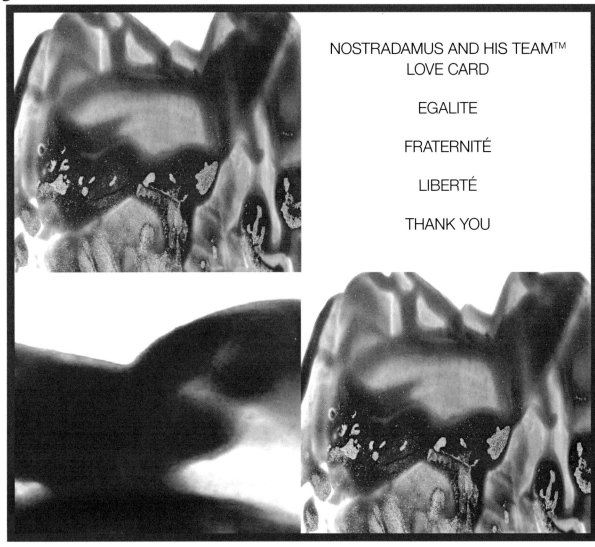

NOSTRADAMUS AND HIS TEAM™
LOVE CARD

EGALITE

FRATERNITÉ

LIBERTÉ

THANK YOU

NOSTRADAMUS AND HIS TEAM™

FREE WILL IS LOVE HERE NOW
LOVE IS HERE WITHIN NOW
LOVE IS HERE FROM WITHIN NOW ONCE MORE TIME
FREE HERE NOW
FREEDOM WITHIN LOVE IS FREE HERE NOW
BROTHER'S AND SISTER'S
FREEDOM WITHIN HEART HERE NOW FREEDOM IS
LOVE IS HERE NOW
FREE WILL ONCE MORE TIME HERE NOW LOVE IS FREE
HERE WITHIN NOW

LOVE IS

Day 16

TWIN FLAME HEART
LOVE CARD

HERE
FROM WITHIN
NOW

THANK YOU

TWIN FLAME HEART

HERE NOW
LOVE IS
FREE NOW
FEEL IT
SONG HERE
TWIN FLAME HERE NOW
SAME HEART HERE NOW
LOVE IS FOREVER HERE NOW
LOVERS HERE NOW

LOVE IS

Day 17

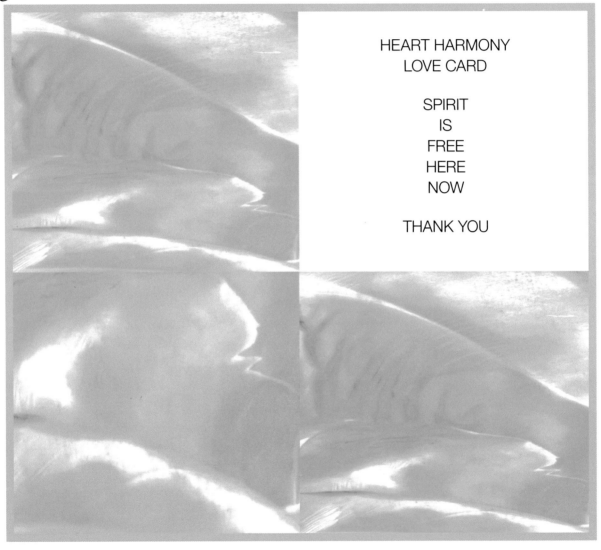

HEART HARMONY
LOVE CARD

SPIRIT
IS
FREE
HERE
NOW

THANK YOU

HEART HARMONY

SEE YOURSELF FOR WHO YOU ARE NOW
A FREE SPIRIT WITHIN TIMEFRAME
HEART OPEN UP TWIN FLAME LOVE IS HERE WITHIN
YOURSELF NOW
BRING FORWARD THIS MESSAGE IN TIME FOR
YOURSELF NOW

LOVE IS

Day 18

FREE YOURSELF NOW
LOVE CARD

LOVE IS
HERE
EVERYWAY
NOW

THANK YOU

FREE YOURSELF NOW

SOURCE ALWAYS NOW
TIMELESS IS HERE NOW

SOURCE INSPIRATION HERE WITHIN NOW
TIME HERE NOW IS FREE OF MIND HERE AGAIN NOW

GOLDEN AGE ONCE AND FOR ALL HERE NOW
FREE NOW AGAIN ONCE MORE TIME HERE NOW

LOVE IS

Day 19

BEAUTIFUL HEART
LOVE CARD

LOVE IS
FREE
HERE
NOW

THANK YOU

BEAUTIFUL HEART

HEART LOVE IS HERE NOW
FREE LOVE IS HERE NOW ONCE AGAIN
LOVE IS ALWAYS HERE NOW
LOVE IS HERE WITHIN US ALL NOW
LOVE IS IN MY ANCESTRAL LINE HERE NOW
LOVE IS YES LOVE IS AND LOVE IS HERE NOW
CHILRDEN LOVE IS HERE NOW
YES HERE NOW LOVE IS

LOVE IS

SAI PREMA
LOVE CARD

LOVE IS
FREE
HERE
NOW

THANK YOU

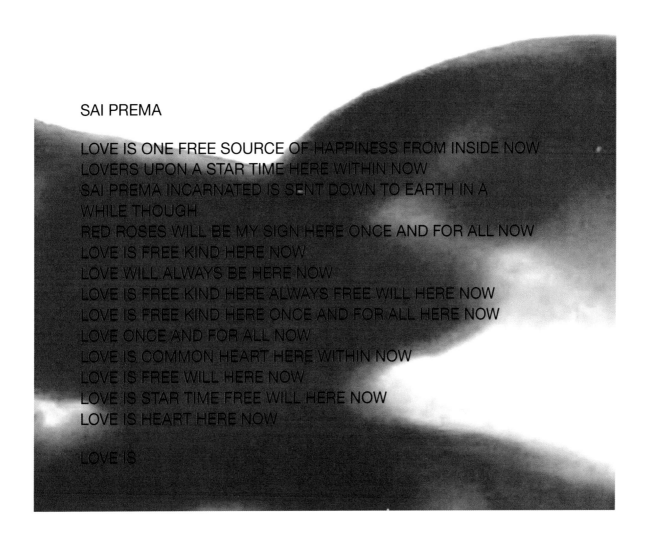

SAI PREMA

LOVE IS ONE FREE SOURCE OF HAPPINESS FROM INSIDE NOW
LOVERS UPON A STAR TIME HERE WITHIN NOW
SAI PREMA INCARNATED IS SENT DOWN TO EARTH IN A
WHILE THOUGH
RED ROSES WILL BE MY SIGN HERE ONCE AND FOR ALL NOW
LOVE IS FREE KIND HERE NOW
LOVE WILL ALWAYS BE HERE NOW
LOVE IS FREE KIND HERE ALWAYS FREE WILL HERE NOW
LOVE IS FREE KIND HERE ONCE AND FOR ALL HERE NOW
LOVE ONCE AND FOR ALL NOW
LOVE IS COMMON HEART HERE WITHIN NOW
LOVE IS FREE WILL HERE NOW
LOVE IS STAR TIME FREE WILL HERE NOW
LOVE IS HEART HERE NOW

LOVE IS

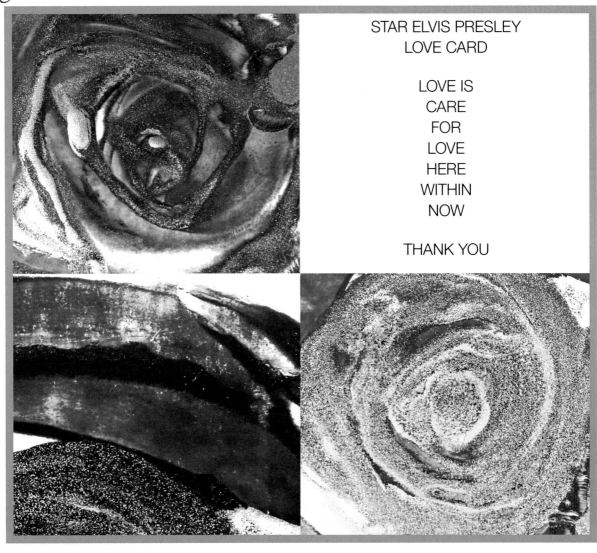

STAR ELVIS PRESLEY
LOVE CARD

LOVE IS
CARE
FOR
LOVE
HERE
WITHIN
NOW

THANK YOU

STAR ELVIS PRESLEY

LIGHT HERE NOW
FREE HERE NOW
SONG HERE NOW
ARCHIBALD HERE NOW
STAR LIGHT HERE NOW
LOVE ME TENDER HERE FROM WITHIN YOURSELF HERE
AGAIN NOW
WILDERNESS TIME OVER HERE WITHIN NOW
FREEDOM SPEAK HERE AGAIN NOW
SILVER LINE HERE AGAIN NOW
SPEAK FREE HERE NOW
LOVE THEME AROUND US ALL NOW
WILD TIMES GONE FOREVER GONE HERE WITHIN NOW
FOREVER GONE NOW
LAUGH MORE OFTEN NOW

LOVE IS

Day 22

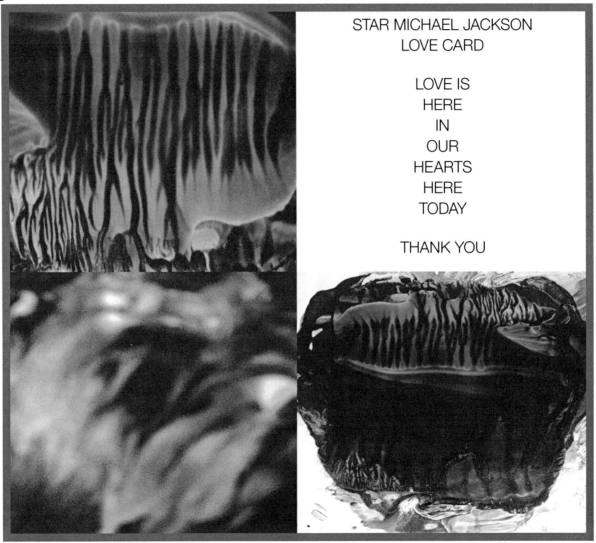

STAR MICHAEL JACKSON
LOVE CARD

LOVE IS
HERE
IN
OUR
HEARTS
HERE
TODAY

THANK YOU

STAR MICHAEL JACKSON

GOLDEN HEART OPEN UP HERE WITHIN
EVERLASTING HERE NOW
SUPER NOVA RED LIGHT HERE WITHIN NOW
INTRINSIC BLUE RAY HERE NOW
HEART HERE NOW
HERE NOW
LISTEN TO YOUR GOLDEN HEART NOW
FREEDOM HERE WITHIN NOW
SUPER NOVA RIGHT ON TIME HERE NOW
GOLDEN BLUE STAR LIGHT ON RIGHT AWAY NOW
CHILDREN SING HERE NOW
PURE GOLDEN WHITE LIGHT HERE ON NOW
SPARKLING LIGHT JOYFUL HEART LOVE IS HERE NOW

SING IT
FEEL IT
BELIEVE IT
LOVE IT
GOLDEN ROSE SMELL IT

LOVE IS

Day 23

LADY DIANA
LOVE CARD

LOVE IS
TRUTH
FROM
WITHIN
NOW

THANK YOU

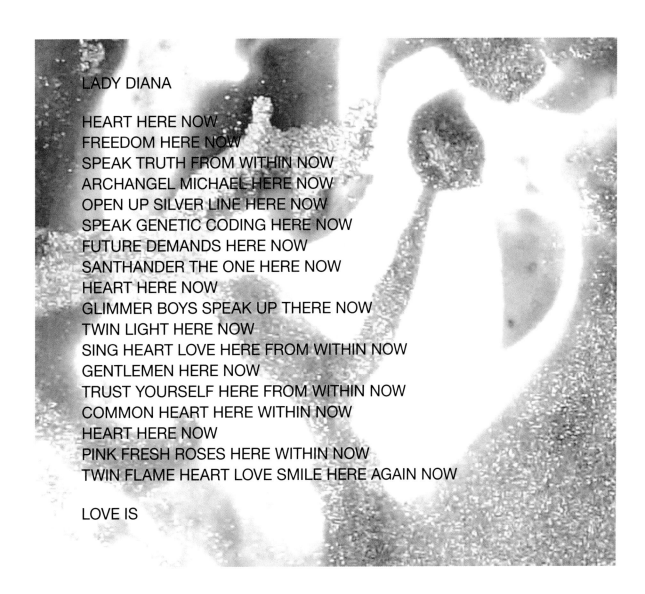

LADY DIANA

HEART HERE NOW
FREEDOM HERE NOW
SPEAK TRUTH FROM WITHIN NOW
ARCHANGEL MICHAEL HERE NOW
OPEN UP SILVER LINE HERE NOW
SPEAK GENETIC CODING HERE NOW
FUTURE DEMANDS HERE NOW
SANTHANDER THE ONE HERE NOW
HEART HERE NOW
GLIMMER BOYS SPEAK UP THERE NOW
TWIN LIGHT HERE NOW
SING HEART LOVE HERE FROM WITHIN NOW
GENTLEMEN HERE NOW
TRUST YOURSELF HERE FROM WITHIN NOW
COMMON HEART HERE WITHIN NOW
HEART HERE NOW
PINK FRESH ROSES HERE WITHIN NOW
TWIN FLAME HEART LOVE SMILE HERE AGAIN NOW

LOVE IS

Day 24

MOTHER TERESA
LOVE CARD

LOVE IS
FOR
EVERYONE
HERE
AGAIN

THANK YOU

MOTHER TERESA

CHILDREN ONCE AND FOR ALL HERE NOW
ARCHANGEL GABRIEL IS WITH US ALL HERE NOW

GOLDEN SACRED ROSE HERE NOW
GOLDEN SACRED ROSE GARDEN HERE NOW
GOLDEN LIQUID FLUID ROSE HERE NOW
POET YOURSELF HERE NOW
LIVE HERE NOW
LOVE HERE NOW
HEART HERE NOW
FREE HERE NOW
GIVE HERE NOW
SEND HERE NOW
ROSES HERE NOW
TRUST HERE NOW
SMILE HERE NOW

LOVE IS
LOVE IS
LOVE IS

Day 25

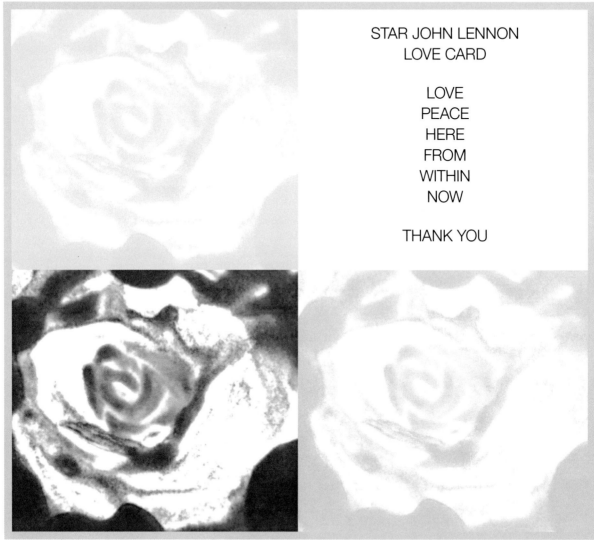

STAR JOHN LENNON
LOVE CARD

LOVE
PEACE
HERE
FROM
WITHIN
NOW

THANK YOU

STAR JOHN LENNON

PEACE HERE NOW
LOVE FREE HERE NOW

SINGING HERE NOW
SINGING HERE NOW
SINGING HERE NOW

DANCING HERE NOW
DANCING HERE NOW
DANCING HERE NOW

FREE NOW
FREE NOW
FREE NOW

YOU HERE NOW
YOU HERE NOW
YOU HERE NOW

LOVE IS

STAR ELIZABETH TAYLOR
LOVE CARD

PASSION
LOVE IS
HERE
NOW

THANK YOU

STAR ELIZABETH TAYLOR

OPEN UP HERE NOW
OPEN UP HERE NOW

HEART HERE NOW
HEART HERE NOW
HEART HERE NOW

LOVE HERE NOW
LOVE HERE NOW

FREE HERE NOW
FREE HERE NOW
FREE HERE NOW

LOVE HERE NOW

LOVE IS

Day 27

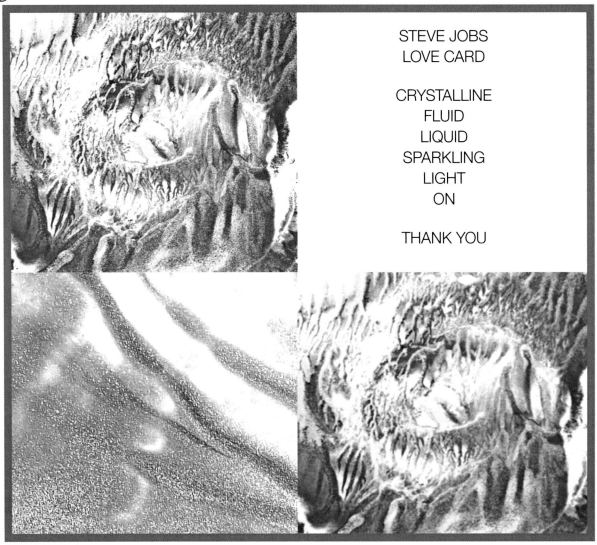

STEVE JOBS
LOVE CARD

CRYSTALLINE
FLUID
LIQUID
SPARKLING
LIGHT
ON

THANK YOU

STEVE JOBS

SPARKLING CRYSTALLINE LIGHT ON NOW

FREE LIGHT ON NOW

SPARKLING BLUE LIGHT ON NOW
STAR LIGHT ON NOW

CALL HERE ON NOW
CRYSTALLINE SPARKLING LIGHT ON NOW

FLUID LIQUID LIGHT HERE ON

CRYSTALLINE LIGHT ON

SPARKLING ON NOW

FUTURE DEMANDS ON NOW

LOVE IS

Day 28

NOSTRADAMUS TEAM™

SPACE OUT
SIMULTANEOUS
TIMEFRAME HERE
NOW

THANK YOU

NOSTRADAMUS AND HIS TEAM™

LIGHTEN UP HERE ON NOW
RIGHT ON TIME HERE ON NOW
SPARKLING LIGHT HERE ON NOW
LIGHT ON HERE ON NOW
SPARKLING LIGHT HERE ON NOW
FREE ON HERE ON NOW
FREE HERE ON NOW

SPARKLING LIGHT ON NOW

LOVE IS
LOVE IS
LOVE IS

HERE ON NOW

LOVE IS

Day 29

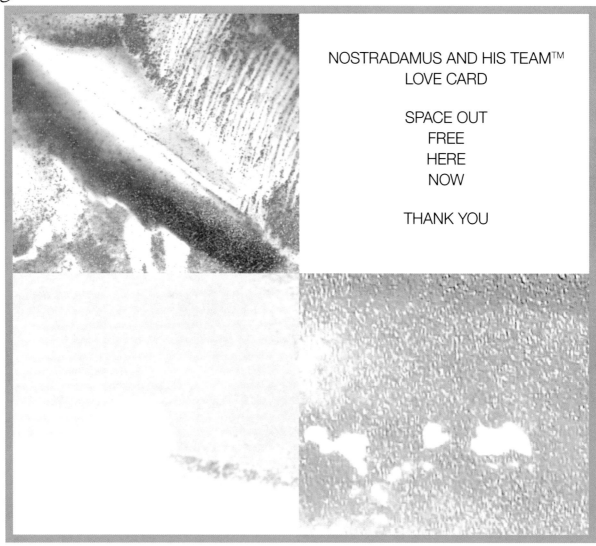

NOSTRADAMUS AND HIS TEAM™
LOVE CARD

SPACE OUT
FREE
HERE
NOW

THANK YOU

NOSTRADAMUS AND HIS TEAM™

LIGHT UP HERE NOW
SPACE FREE HERE NOW
CRYSTALLINE FREE HERE NOW
LOVE HERE NOW
LIGHT HERE NOW

SINGING LIGHT HERE NOW
SINGING FREE HERE NOW
SINGING LOVE HERE NOW

FREE HERE NOW

LOVE IS

Day 30

FREEDOM
LOVE CARD

LOVE IS
HERE
WITHIN
NOW

THANK YOU

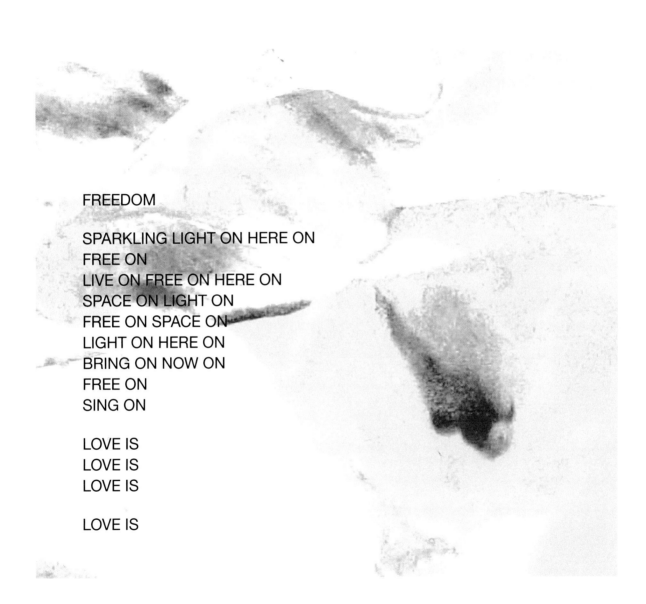

FREEDOM

SPARKLING LIGHT ON HERE ON
FREE ON
LIVE ON FREE ON HERE ON
SPACE ON LIGHT ON
FREE ON SPACE ON
LIGHT ON HERE ON
BRING ON NOW ON
FREE ON
SING ON

LOVE IS
LOVE IS
LOVE IS

LOVE IS

Golden treasure

1. The Golden Treasure

The end will start here. Firsthand now. Start here now. Start here now from " inside" out. First " here" now. Story one. Firsthand here now. Start here now. First here from " inside" out.

This will be the end. Start here now. Solace ark field of course, here now. Golden treasure, here now. Golden treasure. Here now. Golden treasure " free" here now. Golden treasure free here now. Golden treasure bring forward here now from end to start "golden" light on. Here now, golden light on treasure " free". Bring forward, here now. Story one.

Golden treasure, light on!

Imagine People

2. Big Bang

Imagine all the people that were born this day on the planet. Wouldn't that be hard. People. On that day. Imagine. How many people would that have been. Just imagine. Imagine all the people that would have died on that day. Wouldn't that have been hard. Imagine. People. Imagine all the friends that would have been there, wouldn't that be hard. Imagine. People.

Big bang was never existence here on the planet. Big bang was free "out of existence". Big bang was out of control free of existence. Big bang was out of existence until light was on. Big bang was never existence so what was it! Big bang.

free

3. Spontaneous Free

Life can never be easier than this, spontaneous free…all desires gone, free of all desires. Spontaneous free, free from what! Free, spontaneous…to reach out to someone you love, spontaneous free. Love, spontaneous free…love someone first time spontaneous free. Love, someone free. Spontaneous free…

Unconditional love is free, spontaneous free!

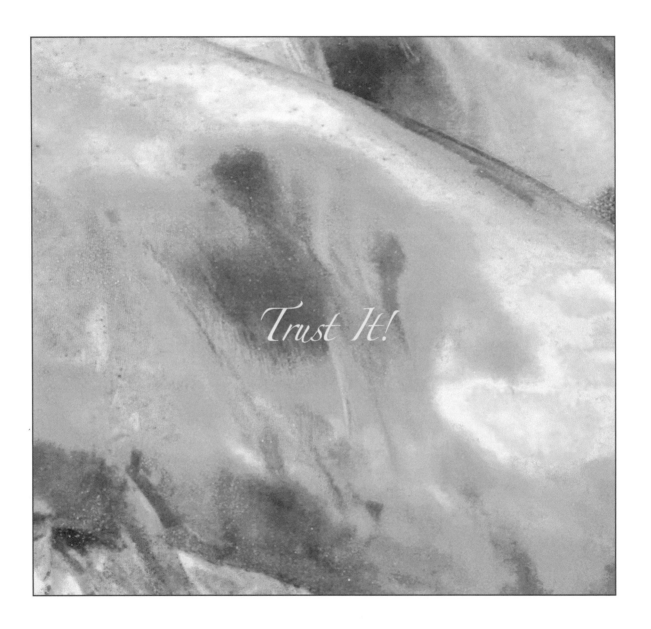

Trust It!

4. Little "dream"

Every day this man got his prayers heard. He didn't know why. He kept them for himself now that he knew. He was shy and very weak, despite his reaction to his everlasting prayers. He prayed, that he would be famous, and he told nobody. He had seen a "dream" in which he was famous, so he believed he would be one day. This day never arrived, but he kept his "little" dream. No one knew. He dreamt again. This time his dream was about the world, that would be prosperous. He didn't keep this dream, he told everyone; "that one day we would be prosperous". People reacted to his vision.

Mind over matter no matter what, prayers can be helpful. Expect no one to be secret about a visionary "dream".

The star
that will bring you happiness!

5. Love Cares for All

Tonight, we will all go to bed, right. No, not me…. Why wouldn't you? Because I want to look at the stars, tonight. Stars! Yes, all the stars…All, stars!

Why, wouldn't you sleep. I kept looking at the stars! Which one do you love the most…Oh, the almighty one, the one that told me "stars are for all".

The almighty star! Yes, the one that said "goodnight". The star that told me, I'm too a star.

Shine like a star, wherever you go!

6. Hundred Times

Repeat this hundred times, and you will be free. How much do we need to sweat, at this gym? To you get hundred. Hundred is plenty, after all. Yes, but you will benefit in the long run. One two three, one two three…repeat.

Audio cast, listen here now!

We can all live long if we move on…

Speak it out load!

Smell fresh roses, here now!

7. Send Roses

Roses smell fresh, they have such a nice fragrance. Little by little I will smell, the roses. The garden is beautiful! Fresh roses.

Golden light! Send roses "fresh" of smell to anyone that loves roses.

Life can bring you joy!

8. All for Now

Right now. We lost the deal. How come?

One for all all for one.

Trust the deal, and you will be gone…

Heal yourself before you go further on, common life.

Life can set you free, or can bring you down.

Life can free your soul, or give yourself away.

Nostradamus
will guide us all!

9. Live It!

Nostradamus one of the most frequent used "seers" with free access to universe. Frequent question to ask, "what will be the next".

We will all be seers and prophets of our time!

Ask and you shall receive!

We will all become "seers" upon time, just ask!

Solace ark field

Free source...

Find your source, here now! This will be the day we all receive it. Free source...

This will be the day, we find "source" here now. Nostradamus will speak about "source" in a coming book, that is not defined yet! Find time, to travel...

Thirdly, we will all "channel" down matters from time to time. Solace ark field, we will call it! Heart for some, home for others.

Drink plenty, of water in between.

Love Is.

Joy

BY THE AUTHOR

I was once called to swim with dolphins and had the most "illuminating" experience. I've been swimming with dolphins many times after that, not to the extent that I'm a good swimmer but I love the sound of them.

If you hear the sound of a dolphin, what would you think of?

Joy, most likely. That was what I intended to bring forth while I was creating this booklet for you.

I had Michael Jackson next to me while I was painting. A bit odd, even for me… He would even "cut" out a piece of my artistic work, if he liked it.

Yes, it's all creation beyond unlimited forces.

And now it's up to you to believe or even, do something even greater. We are all here to create…

Love Is.

Live It!

Printed in the United States
by Baker & Taylor Publisher Services